**FRIENDS
OF ACPL**

First Facts™

Exploring the Animal Kingdom

Insects

two-spotted ladybird beetle

by Adele Richardson

Consultant:
Robert T. Mason
Professor of Zoology, J. C. Braly Curator of Vertebrates
Oregon State University
Corvallis, Oregon

Capstone
press

Mankato, Minnesota

First Facts is published by Capstone Press,
151 Good Counsel Drive, P.O. Box 669, Mankato, Minnesota 56002.
www.capstonepress.com

Library of Congress Cataloging-in-Publication Data
Richardson, Adele, 1966–
    Insects / by Adele Richardson
    p. cm.—(First facts. Exploring the animal kingdom)
    Includes bibliographical references and index.
    ISBN 0-7368-2623-8 (hardcover)
    ISBN 0-7368-4946-7 (paperback)
    1. Insects—Juvenile literature. I. Title. II. Series.
QL467.2.R525 2005
595.7—dc22   2004000670

Summary: Discusses the characteristics, eating habits, and offspring of insects,
    one of the main groups in the animal kingdom.

Editorial credits
Erika L. Shores, editor; Linda Clavel, designer; Kelly Garvin, photo researcher;
    Eric Kudalis, product planning editor

Photo credits
Brand X Pictures/Burke/Triolo, cover (all)
Bruce Coleman Inc./J. C. Carton, 6–7; Michael Black, 9; Wardene Weisser, 20
Corel, 17
Digital Vision/Gerry Ellis and Michael Durham, 1, 16
Dwight R. Kuhn, 12–13, 19 (all)
Eda Rogers, 15
McDonald Wildlife Photography/Joe McDonald, 11

1 2 3 4 5 6 09 08 07 06 05 04

Table of Contents

Insects

Insects belong to the animal kingdom. Butterflies, ladybugs, and ants are insects.

Other groups of animals live on earth with insects. Mammals have hair. Birds have feathers. Reptiles have hard, dry skin. Amphibians have moist skin. Fish have fins.

Birds

Mammals

Reptiles

Main Animal Groups

Insects

Amphibians

Fish

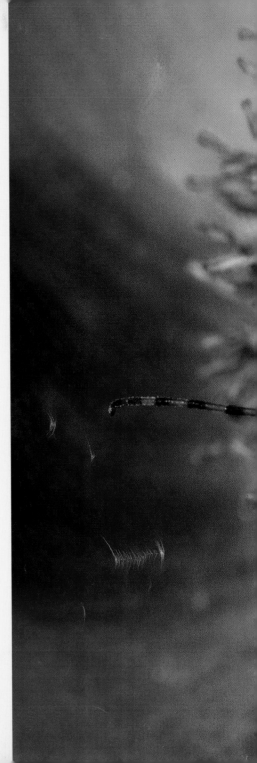

Insects Are Invertebrates

Insects do not have any bones inside their bodies. Insects are **invertebrates**. Invertebrates do not have backbones. Instead, insects have a hard outer covering called an **exoskeleton**. A beetle's exoskeleton covers its soft body.

long-horned beetle

Insects Are Cold-Blooded

Insects are cold-blooded animals. Their body temperatures change with their surroundings. Most insects are more active in warm temperatures. This fly's body temperature is too cold. It rests in the sun to warm up.

Fun Fact!

Insects do not have red blood. Their blood is colorless or a yellow-green color.

tachinid fly

Bodies of Insects

Insects have three main body parts. They are the head, the **thorax**, and the **abdomen**. Most insects have body parts like this wasp. Its head has eyes, a mouth, and **antennae**. Wings and six legs join to its middle part called the thorax. The end part is the abdomen.

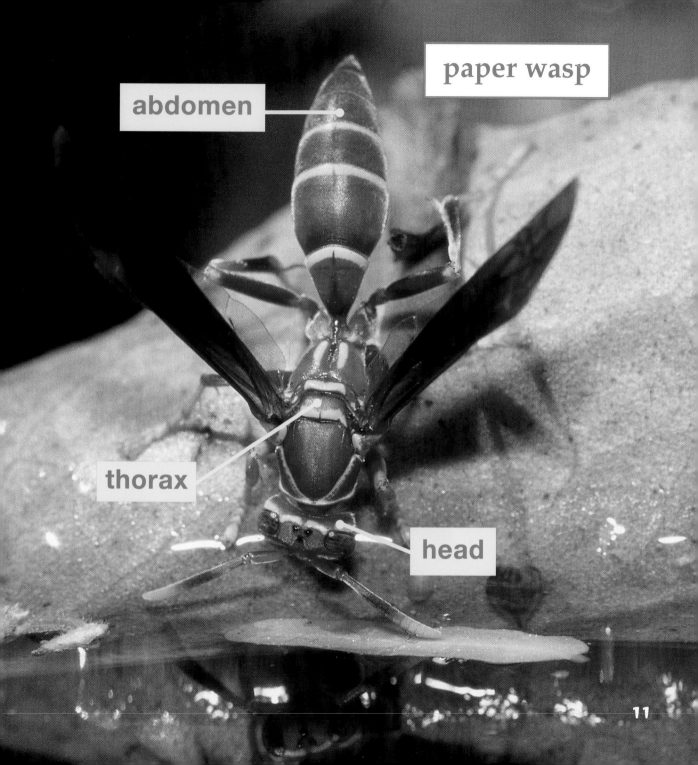

abdomen

paper wasp

thorax

head

Insects Have Hard Skin

An insect's exoskeleton is hard skin. It is mostly made of **chitin**. Tiny hairs or spines often grow from the chitin.

The exoskeleton does not grow with an insect. A grasshopper sheds its old skin as it grows. New skin grows in its place.

Fun Fact!
Some insects have tiny hairs all over their bodies, including on their eyes.

How Insects Breathe

Insects breathe air with **spiracles**. Spiracles are tiny openings on an insect's body. A butterfly has spiracles along the sides of its abdomen. Insects can close each spiracle. They keep water from going into their bodies.

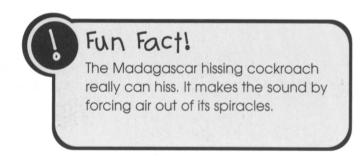

Fun Fact!

The Madagascar hissing cockroach really can hiss. It makes the sound by forcing air out of its spiracles.

cairns birdwing butterfly

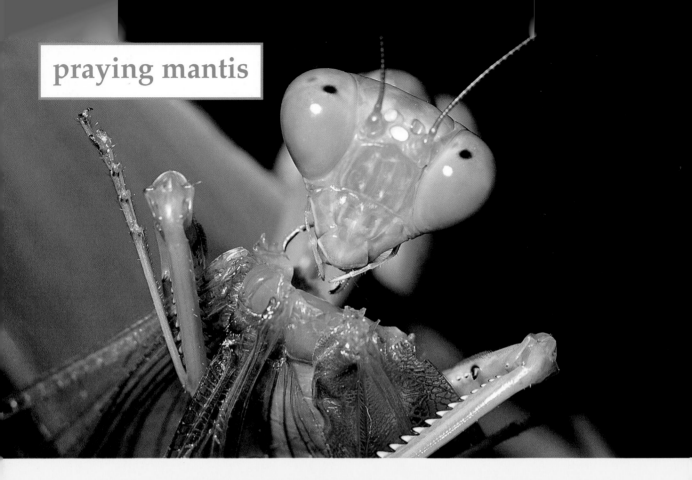

praying mantis

What Insects Eat

Insects eat different kinds of food. Some insects eat plants. Some insects eat other insects. This praying mantis chews on a large insect.

long-horned beetle

Most insects have strong jaws for
chewing. Their jaws move side to side.
Their jaws do not move up and down
like a person's jaws do.

Life Cycle

Insects either are born live or **hatch** from eggs. Insects that hatch from eggs go through changes to become adults. A newly hatched moth looks like a worm. It is called a caterpillar. It spins a **cocoon** around its body. The moth breaks out of its cocoon after it changes into an adult.

hatching luna moth caterpillar

luna moth cocoon

luna moth

Amazing but True!

Insects help make silk fabric. Silkworms spin cocoons around their bodies. People unwind the silk. One thread can be 13,000 feet (3,962 meters) long. People spin and weave the threads together to make fabric.

Compare the Main Animal Groups

	Vertebrates	Invertebrates	Warm-blooded	Cold-blooded	Hair	Feathers	Scales
Insects		X		X			
Amphibians	X			X			
Birds	X		X			X	
Fish	X			X			X
Mammals	X		X		X		
Reptiles	X			X			X

Glossary

abdomen (AB-duh-muhn)—the end section of an insect's body

antennae (an-TEN-ee)—feelers on an insect's head

chitin (KY-ten)—one of the hard materials making up an exoskeleton

cocoon (kuh-KOON)—a covering made from silky threads

exoskeleton (ek-soh-SKE-luh-tuhn)—the hard outer shell of an insect

hatch (HACH)—to break out of an egg

invertebrate (in-VUR-tuh-bruht)—an animal without a backbone

spiracles (SPEER-uh-kuhlss)—tiny holes through which some animals breathe

thorax (THOR-aks)—the middle section of an insect's body; wings and legs are attached to the thorax.

Read More

Pike, Katy. *Insects.* Animal Facts. Philadelphia: Chelsea Clubhouse Books, 2003.

Schaefer, Lola M. *What Is an Insect?* The Animal Kingdom. Mankato, Minn.: Pebble Books, 2001.

Internet Sites

FactHound offers a safe, fun way to find Internet sites related to this book. All of the sites on FactHound have been researched by our staff.

Here's how:
1. Visit *www.facthound.com*
2. Type in this special code **0736826238** for age-appropriate sites. Or enter a search word related to this book for a more general search.
3. Click on the **Fetch It** button.

FactHound will fetch the best sites for you!

Index